Explore new ideas!

Welcome to your Reading/Writing **Workshop**

Read exciting literature, science and social studies texts!

Become an expert writer!

Build vocabulary and knowledge to unlock the Wonders of reading!

Use your student login to explore your interactive Reading/Writing Workshop, practice close reading, and more.

Go Digital! www.connected.mcgraw-hill.com

(tl) Iñaki Relanzon/naturepl.com; (rt) Andy Rouse/The Image Bank/Getty Images; (rb) Daniel Moreton; (b) Nathan Love

Program Authors

Diane August

Donald R. Bear

Janice A. Dole

Jana Echevarria

Douglas Fisher

David Francis

Vicki Gibson

Jan Hasbrouck

Margaret Kilgo

Jay McTighe

Scott G. Paris

Timothy Shanahan

Josefina V. Tinajero

Mc
Graw
Hill
Education

Cover and Title pages: Nathan Love

www.mheonline.com/readingwonders

Send all inquiries to:
McGraw-Hill Education
2 Penn Plaza
New York, NY 10121

ISBN: 978-0-07-677113-4
MHID: 0-07-677113-X

Printed in the United States of America.

4 5 6 7 8 9 QVS 20 19 18 17 16

A

Unlock the Wonders of Reading

With your *Reading/Writing Workshop* you will:

- Read and Reread Exciting Literature and Informational Text

- Have Collaborative Conversations with Partners

- Learn to Unlock Complex Text

- Understand What a Good Writer Does

Get Ready to Become:

- A Strong Reader

- A Good Speaker and Listener

- An Expert Writer

READ and REREAD

Exciting Literature

Adventure stories and fantasies will take you to new worlds! Through poems and folktales you can discover many new wonders. It's all waiting for you!

Informational Texts

Read about brave people and amazing animals. Learn some surprising facts. Informational texts will open up the worlds of Science and Social Studies to you!

ACT
Access Complex Text

When you read, take notes on what you don't understand. The questions below will help you read any text.

VOCABULARY

What if don't know a word? I can look for context clues. I can use a dictionary.

CONNECT IDEAS

Can I connect ideas from one part of the text to another? This can help me better understand the text.

TEXT FEATURES

Does the selection have pictures, maps, or diagrams? They can help, too!

TEXT STRUCTURE

Knowing how a text is organized will help me understand what I am reading.

COLLABORATE

What do you do when you don't understand something that you read?

Look for Text Evidence

You can look for clues in the text to answer a question. That's called text evidence. Read like an explorer and discover the clues!

Hundreds of barracuda fish swim in a school together.

Stated
How many barracuda fish swim together?
The answer is right there!

Fish in a school keep each other safe.

Unstated
How can fish help each other?
Here is my clue!

Text Evidence

Sometimes you will find answers right there in the text. Sometimes you need to look for clues in different parts of the text.

It's Stated — Right There!

Some questions ask you to find details, like: How many barracuda fish swim together? You can point to the answer in the text.

It's Not Stated — But Here's My Evidence!

Think of a question like: How can fish help each other? To answer it, you look for a clue. Then you put the clue in your own words to answer the question.

 What evidence in the text tells why it's a good idea for fish to swim in schools?

Be an Expert Writer!

Good readers are good writers. When you read a text closely, you see what an expert writer does. Good writing is organized, has clear ideas, and contains details. See how David learned to write an informative text.

David's Model

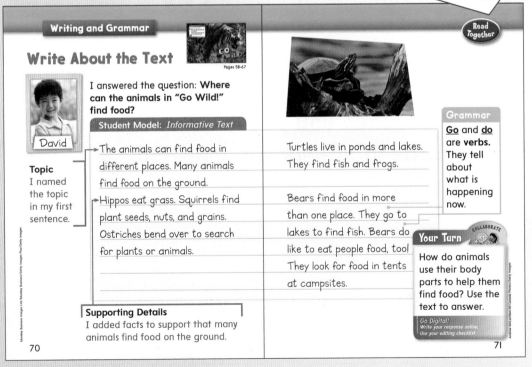

Write About the Text

You can write about something that you have read closely. Introduce your topic and use details from the text to tell about the topic. Use the checklist below.

Opinion Did I name my topic? Did I state my opinion and explain my reasons for my opinion? Did I write a concluding sentence?

Informative Texts Did I name my topic and include some facts about it? Is my concluding sentence strong?

Narrative Texts Did I tell about the events in order? Did I use some time-order words? Are there details that help the reader understand what is happening? Do I have a strong ending?

 What do you like to write about?

Unit 4

Animals Everywhere

The Big Idea

What animals do you know about? What are they like? **10**

(b) Valeria Cis

4

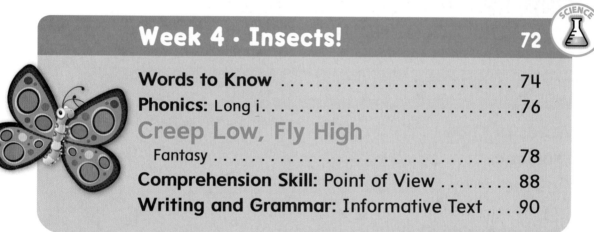
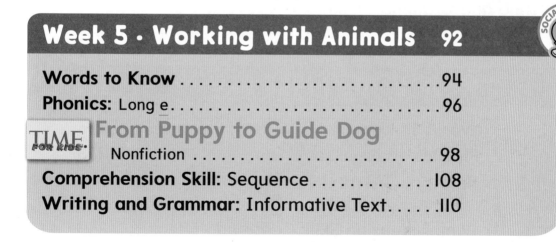
SCIENCE

SCIENCE

SOCIAL STUDIES

TIME FOR KIDS

(t) Andy Rouse/The Image Bank/Getty Images; (b) Daniel Moreton

5

Unit 5

Figure It Out

The Big Idea

How can we make sense of the world around us?........ **112**

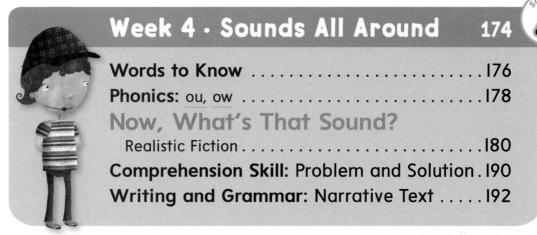
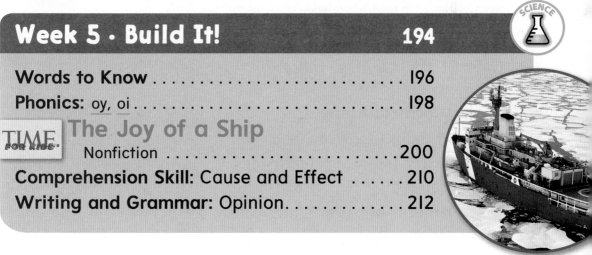
SOCIAL STUDIES

SCIENCE

SCIENCE

TIME FOR KIDS®

(t) Pablo Bernasconi; (b) USCG photo by Patrick Kelley

Unit 6

Together We Can!

The Big Idea

How does teamwork help us? 214

(t) Gynux; (b) Masterfile

Go Digital! www.connected.mcgraw-hill.com

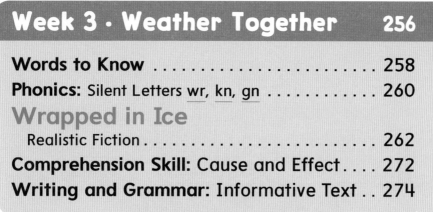

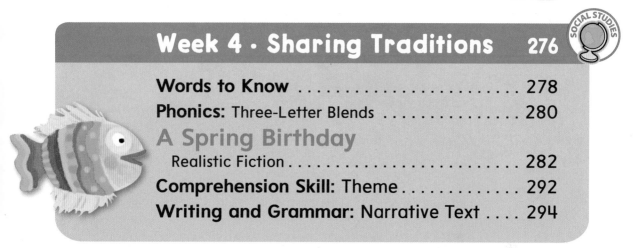

Animals Everywhere

The Big Idea

What animals do you know about? What are they like?

Animals on the Go

Animals are on the go,
Some moving fast, some moving slow.

Crabs and spiders like to crawl,
A turtle hardly moves at all.

Elephants stomp when they pass,
But snakes just slither through the grass.

Kangaroos and rabbits hop,
BOING BOING BOUNCE—

      Do they EVER stop?

—by Allegra Perrot

Essential Question

How do animals' bodies help them?

Go Digital!

Creature Features

Talk About It

What part of the body is helping these giraffes?

about

Did you see this book **about** bats?

animal

This **animal** has a trunk.

carry

It's easy to **carry** a little pet.

eight

A spider has **eight** legs.

give

I **give** my dog some water.

our

Our parrots like to talk.

special

Penguins move in a **special** way.

splendid

A peacock has a **splendid** tail.

(t to b, l to r) SVGiles/Flickr Open/Getty Images; Jack Weinberg/Image Source/ PunchStock; Image Source/PunchStock; imagebroker.net/SuperStock; Juniors Bildarchiv/age fotostock; IT Stock/PunchStock/Getty Images; Digital Vision/Getty Images; Corbis/SuperStock

COLLABORATE

Your Turn

Read the sentence for each word. Then make up another sentence.

Go Digital! Use the online visual glossary

Long a

The letters a, ai, and ay make the long a sound in **apron**, **paint**, and **gray**.

may	play	days
paid	stained	trains
clay	mail	staying
April	agent	basic

Will David stay inside if it rains?

David and Ray may play with trains.

Your Turn

COLLABORATE

Look for these words with long a in "A Tale of a Tail."

tail	Ray	day
April	swayed	way
wailed	explained	

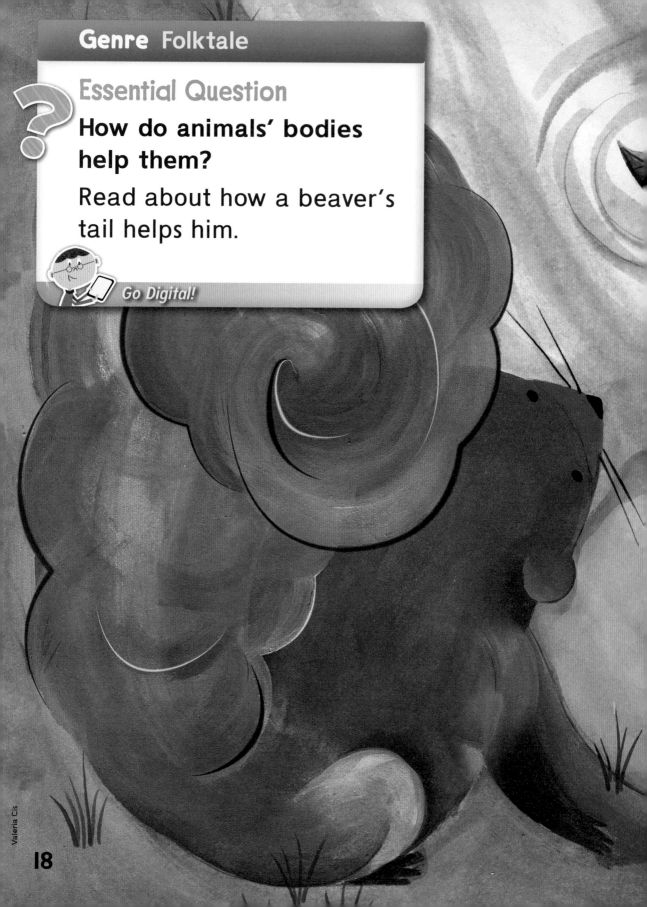

Essential Question

How do animals' bodies help them?

Read about how a beaver's tail helps him.

Go Digital!

Valeria Cis

18

A Tale of a Tail

Long ago, there lived a beaver named Ray.

Ray was quite proud of his nice thick tail. He spent a lot of time brushing and fluffing it.

Valeria Cis

"I have a **splendid** tail," Ray bragged. "It is the best tail that an **animal** can have!"

One fine day in April, Ray went out.

"It is a nice day to chop wood," he said. So Ray got his ax. He chop, chop, chopped a big tree **eight** times.

The big tree swayed this way and that. Then it fell—on top of Ray's tail! Ray tugged and tugged at his tail. He gasped when he pulled it out.

"My tail is flat!" Ray wailed.

The sun looked down at him. She could tell that Ray felt bad **about** his tail.

24

"A flat tail will help you swim fast," the sun explained. "A flat tail can send a signal, too. Just slap it on the water."

That made Ray happy.

"I have a **special** tail!" yelled Ray.

Then Ray slapped his tail on the water. SLAP, SLAP, SLAP!

His pals came running. "Do you want **our** help?" they asked.

Valeria Cis

"I want to **give** you a ride,"
said Ray. "Hop on my tail.
I will **carry** you across the lake."

And happy Ray swam off as fast
as a fish!

Make Connections

How did Ray's new tail
help him?

27

Sequence

The **sequence** is the order of events in a story. Think about what happens first, next, then, and last in the folktale.

 Find Text Evidence

Find out what happens first in the story.

page 20

Long ago, there lived a beaver named Ray.

Ray was quite proud of his nice thick tail. He spent a lot of time brushing and fluffing it.

Valeria Cis

First

Ray likes his thick, bushy tail a lot.

Next

A tree falls and makes Ray's tail flat. He is sad.

Then

The sun explains how a flat tail will help Ray.

Last

Ray's flat tail helps him send a signal, swim fast, and give his pals a ride.

COLLABORATE

Your Turn

Talk about the sequence of events in "A Tale of a Tail."

Go Digital! *Use the interactive graphic organizer*

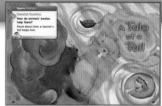

Write About the Text

Pages 18–27

Ana

I responded to the prompt: **Write a tale explaining how the beaver's friend, the bunny, got its ears.**

Student Model: *Narrative Text*

Sequence
I told about the events in an order that makes sense.

Long ago, bunnies had small ears. One day, Ben Bunny saw Ray and the beavers talking. Ben wanted to hear them.

Specific Words
I used **sneak** to describe how Ben moved.

Ben tried to sneak up behind a tree to hear the beavers. When Ben tried to move, his ears got stuck in the branches.

Ben tried to pull his ears free.
His ears were stuck. Ben was
surprised! Then Ray and his
friends came to help. They
pulled Ben's ears out of the
branches.

Ben's ears had stretched.
They were very long.
That is how Ben and
bunnies got such long ears.

Grammar

Was and **were** are **past-tense verbs** that tell about actions that already happened.

Your Turn

COLLABORATE

Write a tale explaining why the beaver's friend, the frog, has a croaky voice.

Go Digital!
Write your response online.
Use your editing checklist.

31

Weekly Concept Animals Together

Essential Question

How do animals help each other?

Go Digital!

Team Up!

Talk About It

How do the bird and the hippo help each other?

because

This team will win **because** it is fast.

blue

The geese fly in the **blue** sky.

into

They go **into** the water together.

or

Do you think the deer will stay **or** run?

other

One animal cleans the **other**.

small

Small ants can carry very big bits.

danger

Mom keeps her cub out of **danger**.

partner

A **partner** is a big help.

Your Turn

COLLABORATE

Read the sentence for each word. Then make up another sentence.

Go Digital! Use the online visual glossary

Long e

The letters e, ee, ea, and ie make the long e sound in **he, bees, eat,** and **chief.**

me	see	each
she	leaf	peek
brief	treated	thief
meeting	green	beast

We peeked at Jean's hives in the field.

She told us, "Each bee works hard."

Your Turn

COLLABORATE

Look for these words with long e in "A Team of Fish."

team	creeks	deep	seas
the	each	eat	be
chief	reason	neat	keep

Essential Question

How do animals help each other?

Read about how some fish help each other.

Go Digital!

Martin Strmiska /Alamy

A Team of Fish

Fish swim in lakes and creeks. Fish swim in deep **blue** seas **or** oceans.

Let's dive **into** the water. Let's look at fish!

Fish can swim alone. Fish can swim with a **partner**.

Fish can swim in a bunch, too. A bunch of fish is called a school.

A school has lots of fish. They are a team.

The fish help each **other**. They look for food together.

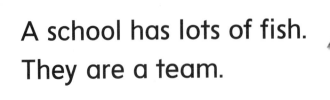

Fish eat lots of things. Some fish eat **small** animals. Some fish eat other fish!

These catfish eat together for safety.

It can be unsafe to swim alone.
What is the chief reason? **Danger!**
A fish can get snapped up!

But a fish can hide in a school.

Fish in a school have a neat trick. The fish swim close together.

Big fish will not mess with them **because** they look like one huge fish.

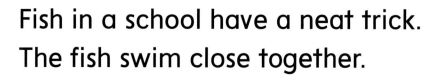

These crescent-tail bigeye fish swim in a school to fool big fish.

This big fish wants to eat. But it stays away. The school looks like a huge fish that may eat him!

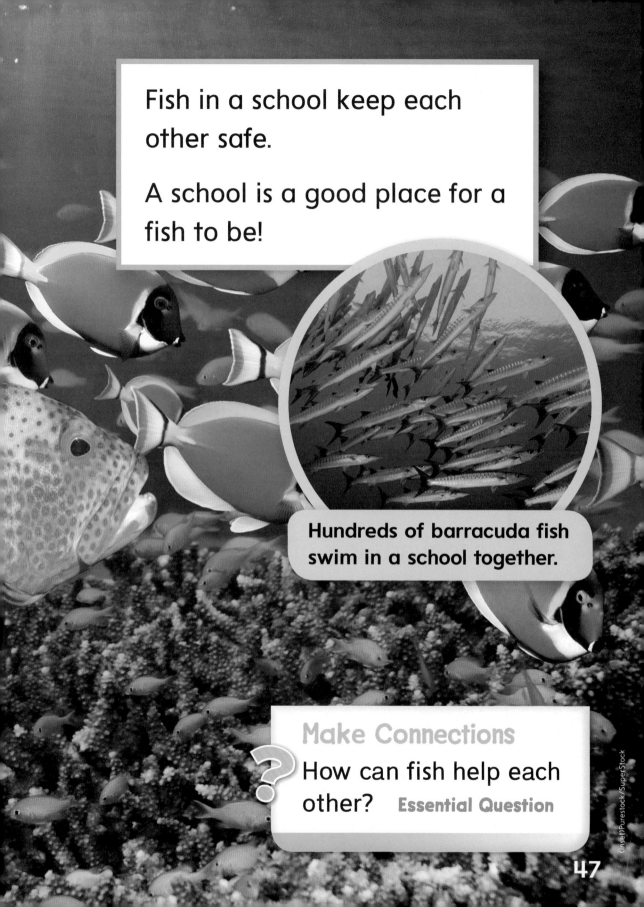

Fish in a school keep each other safe.

A school is a good place for a fish to be!

Hundreds of barracuda fish swim in a school together.

Make Connections

How can fish help each other? **Essential Question**

(inset)Purestock/SuperStock

Main Idea and Key Details

The **main idea** is what the selection is mostly about.

Key details give information about the main idea.

Find Text Evidence

Find a detail about how fish in a school help each other.

page 42

A school has lots of fish.
They are a team.

The fish help each **other**. They look for food together.

Reinhard Dirscherl/Alamy

Main Idea
Fish in a school help each other.

Detail	Detail	Detail
The fish look for food together.	The fish keep each other safe.	They help keep big fish away.

Your Turn

COLLABORATE

Talk about the main idea and details in "A Team of Fish."

Go Digital! *Use the interactive graphic organizer*

Write About the Text

A Team of Fish

Pages 38–47

Andrew

I answered the question: **In your opinion, what are some good and bad things about being a big fish?**

Student Model: *Opinion*

Topic
I wrote the topic and told what I think.

Facts
I supplied a fact about big fish to support my answer.

There are some good things and bad things about being a big fish. I think it's good to be a big fish because it is safer than being a little fish. Other fish are scared of a big fish. When other fish see a big fish, they don't try to eat it.

Jessica lewis/Moment/Getty Images

50

It can also be bad to be a big fish. A big fish swimming alone has to find food on its own. When many little fish swim together, they have many eyes to look for food.

Grammar

The verbs **has** and **have** are used correctly.

COLLABORATE

Your Turn

In your opinion, what are some good things and bad things about being a little fish? Use text evidence in your answer.

Go Digital!
Write your response online.
Use your editing checklist.

Essential Question

How do animals survive in nature?

Go Digital!

52

Survivors!

Talk About It

How does this eagle get food to eat?

find

Fish can **find**
a place to hide.

food

All animals need
food to live.

more

We give it **more**
food to eat.

over

The girl jumps
over the rope.

start

When does a cub
start to walk?

warm

The lion sat in the **warm** sun.

search

Do bees **search** for plants?

seek

A bear will **seek** out ripe berries.

COLLABORATE

Your Turn

Read the sentence for each word. Then make up another sentence.

Go Digital! *Use the online visual glossary*

Long o

The letters o, oa, ow, and oe make the long o sound in **go**, **road**, **crow**, and **doe**.

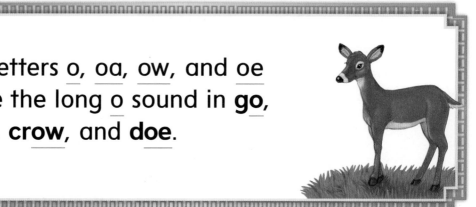

old	boats	showing
Joe	most	groan
slow	toes	told
goes	toasted	window

Joe used soap to clean the bowl.

He soaked it in cold water.

COLLABORATE

Your Turn

Look for these words with long o in "Go Wild!"

go	grow	don't
hippos	hippo	loads
snow	toads	goes
no	so	both
cold	most	

Essential Question

How do animals survive in nature?

Read about how animals in the wild find food.

Go Digital!

EckPhoto/Alamy

GO WILD!

Animals need food to live and grow. But all animals don't eat the same things. Some big animals such as hippos eat plants. A hippo can eat more than 130 pounds of grass!

Richard McManus/Moment/Getty Images

Some small animals eat plants, too. A squirrel eats loads of plant seeds. They like nuts and grains. A squirrel can smell a nut and **find** it even in the snow!

Alex Fieldhouse/Alamy

Some animals hunt and eat other animals. First this big cat runs fast to catch its meal. Then it will use its claws and teeth to eat.

Andy Rouse/The Image Bank/Getty Images

Frogs and toads **seek** insects and snails to eat. A big frog goes after mice, too. But frogs and toads have no teeth. So they must gulp down their meal!

Some animals eat both plants and animals. An ostrich eats seeds and leaves. But it will **search** all **over** for insects, snakes, and lizards as well.

A painted turtle eats plants, fish, and frogs. This reptile lives in lakes and ponds. It likes the cold water at first. But then it will come up on land to get **warm**.

A bear may **start** its day by eating plants. Next, it may go fishing in a lake. After that, a bear may go hunting. Then, it may even go to a campsite.

Most bears will eat plants, animals, and people food. Is there any food left here to eat? If so, a bear will find it! In the wild, animals find food in lots of places.

Make Connections

? What do animals in the wild eat? **Essential Question**

Juniors Bildarchiv/Alamy

Main Idea and Key Details

The **main idea** is what the selection is mostly about.

Key details give information about the main idea.

 Find Text Evidence

Find key details about what animals in the wild eat.

page 60

Animals need **food** to live and grow. But all animals don't eat the same things. Some big animals such as hippos eat plants. A hippo can eat **more** than 130 pounds of grass!

Main Idea

Animals in the wild eat many different things.

Detail

Some animals such as hippos eat plants.

Detail

Some animals such as ostriches eat both plants and animals.

Detail

Some animals such as frogs eat other animals.

Your Turn

COLLABORATE

Talk about the main idea and details in "Go Wild!"

Go Digital! Use the interactive graphic organizer

69

Write About the Text

Pages 58–67

David

I answered the question: **Where can the animals in "Go Wild!" find food?**

Student Model: *Informative Text*

Topic
I named the topic in my first sentence.

The animals can find food in different places. Many animals find food on the ground. Hippos eat grass. Squirrels find plant seeds, nuts, and grains. Ostriches bend over to search for plants or animals.

Supporting Details
I added facts to support that many animals find food on the ground.

Turtles live in ponds and lakes. They find fish and frogs.

Bears find food in more than one place. They go to lakes to find fish. Bears do like to eat people food, too! They look for food in tents at campsites.

Grammar

Go and **do** are **verbs.** They tell about what is happening now.

Your Turn

COLLABORATE

How do animals use their body parts to help them find food? Use the text to answer.

Go Digital!
Write your response online.
Use your editing checklist.

Andrew McLachlan/All Canada Photos/Getty Images

Essential Question

What insects do you know about? How are they alike and different?

Go Digital!

Bug Me!

 Talk About It

What is special about the
caterpillar? How is it
like other bugs?

caught

A bug is **caught** in this web.

flew

The wasp **flew** over to the flower.

know

I **know** how to catch a bug!

laugh

That bug story made us **laugh**.

listen

Listen to the buzzing bees!

were

Fireflies **were** out last night.

beautiful

The butterfly has **beautiful** wings.

fancy

We are wearing **fancy** hats.

Your Turn

COLLABORATE

Read the sentence for each word. Then make up another sentence.

Go Digital! Use the online visual glossary

Long i

The letters i, y, igh, and ie make the long i sound in **find**, **fly**, **high**, and **cries**.

by	untie	sighed
mild	sky	tries
dry	kind	relight
right	child	spied

Dwight spied a moth by the light.

"What kind is it?" I asked myself.

Your Turn

Look for these words with long i in "Creep Low, Fly High."

fly	high	I	sighed
cried	right	find	sky
by	hi	I'm	

Essential Question

What insects do you know about? How are they alike and different?

Read about what some insects are like.

Go Digital!

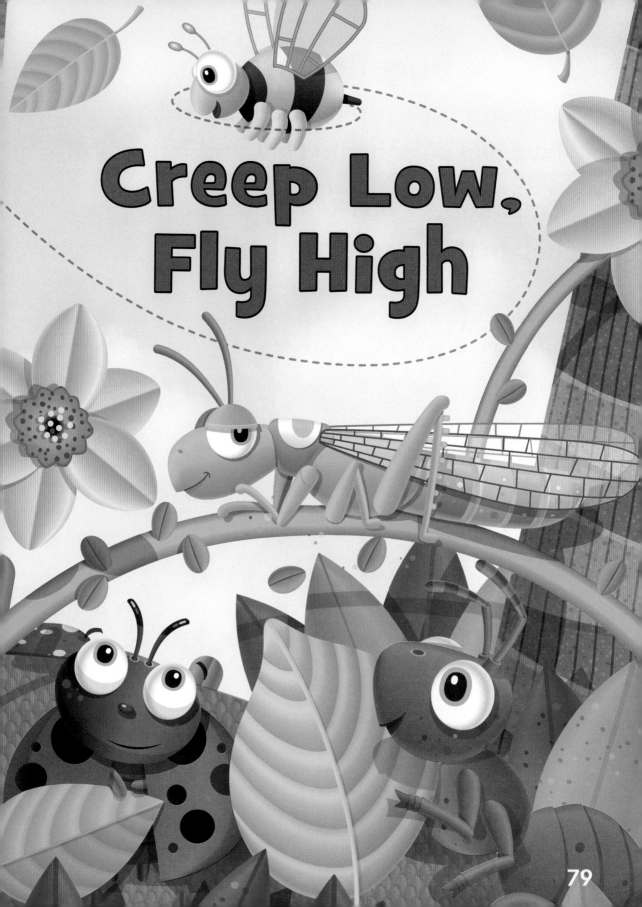

Creep Low, Fly High

Bug Boasts

The sun came up over a big field. Five bug pals met to chat and **laugh**.

Grasshopper boasted a bit. "I can hop to the top of any plant!"

Daniel Moreton

"Well, I can dash fast," bragged Ant.

"**Listen**!" hummed Bee. "I can buzz as I fly high."

"And I can zip around on **fancy** spotted wings!" smiled Ladybug.

"Not I," sighed Caterpillar.
"I just creep, creep, creep."
Then he crept away.

"Come back!" his pals wailed.
But Caterpillar did not.

Missing!

It was time for lunch. The bugs did not see Caterpillar. He was missing! Where did he go?

"I think I **know** where he is!" cried Ant. "He is hiding because he feels bad."

"I think that's right," nodded Grasshopper. "Let's find him. We can cheer him up!"

The two rushed away.

"What if he is not hiding?" asked
Bee. "I saw a bird when we **were**
chatting,"added Bee. "It **flew** low in
the sky."

"What if it **caught** our pal?" cried
Ladybug. "We must find out! Maybe
we can save him!"

The two flew away.

Still a Pal

The bugs did not find Caterpillar. Many days went by. The pals were sad. Then one day they saw a **beautiful** bug with gold wings.

"Hi! I'm back!" the bug called as he flew by. "I wrapped up and rested. Then I popped out like this!"

Daniel Moreton

"It's me—Butterfly! I used to be Caterpillar!" cried Butterfly.

"But you are not the same," sighed Ant.

"But I am still a pal," said Butterfly. "And now I can flit and dip! Let's go have some fun!"

Make Connections

How can insects be alike and different?

Essential Question

Point of View

Point of view is the way that a story character thinks or feels.

🔍 Find Text Evidence

Find the point of view of one of the story characters.

page 84

"I think I **know** where he is!" cried Ant. "He is hiding because he feels bad."

Daniel Moreton

Character	Clue	Point of View
Ant	Thinks that Caterpillar is hiding because he feels bad.	Is worried about Caterpillar.
Ladybug	Thinks that a bird caught Caterpillar.	Wants to save Caterpillar.
Caterpillar/ Butterfly	Tells Ant that he can now flit and dip.	Is happy to be a butterfly who can fly!

Your Turn

COLLABORATE

Talk about the different points of view in "Creep Low, Fly High."

Go Digital! Use the interactive graphic organizer

Write About the Text

Pages 78-87

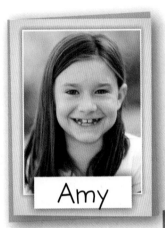

Amy

I answered the question: **How do Caterpillar's looks change from the story's beginning to the end?**

Student Model: *Informative Text*

Compare and Contrast
I told details from the beginning of the story first.

In the beginning of the story,

I see that Caterpillar is colorful.

He is green and yellow. He

has blue dots and red circles.

Caterpillar cannot fly or hop.

He moves slowly on the ground.

He creeps along.

Grammar

See is a **verb** in the present tense.

Rosemarie Gearhart/Vetta/Getty Images

90

Concluding Statement
I wrote how Caterpillar looks different at the end of the story.

At the end of the story, Caterpillar looks different. He has wings. Now he can fly with his pals. He became a butterfly.

Your Turn COLLABORATE

How do Caterpillar's feelings change from the beginning to the end of the story?

Go Digital!
Write your response online.
Use your editing checklist.

91

Essential Question

How do people work with animals?

Go Digital!

Animals and Us

Talk About It

What is the trainer teaching this dog?

found

The dog **found** a bone.

hard

The horses are working **hard**.

near

The dog is **near** the trainer.

woman

The **woman** walks the dog.

would

She **would** like to ride.

write

She will **write** what we need.

clever

This bird is very **clever**!

signal

The trainer gives a **signal**.

COLLABORATE

Your Turn

Read the sentence for each word. Then make up another sentence.

Go Digital! Use the online visual glossary

Long <u>e</u>

The letters <u>y</u> and <u>ey</u> can make the long e sound in **pupp<u>y</u>** and **k<u>ey</u>**.

luck<u>y</u>	all<u>ey</u>	sunn<u>y</u>
budd<u>y</u>	Mick<u>ey</u>	cit<u>y</u>
eas<u>y</u>	penn<u>y</u>	sleep<u>y</u>
grass<u>y</u>	vall<u>ey</u>	health<u>y</u>

Did you lose your k<u>ey</u> in the all<u>ey</u>?

We walk Zigg<u>y</u> when it is sunn<u>y</u>.

COLLABORATE

Your Turn

Look for these words with long e in "From Puppy to Guide Dog."

pupp<u>y</u>	k<u>ey</u>	Mick<u>ey</u>	budd<u>y</u>
laz<u>y</u>	fuss<u>y</u>	health<u>y</u>	cit<u>y</u>
read<u>y</u>	eas<u>y</u>		

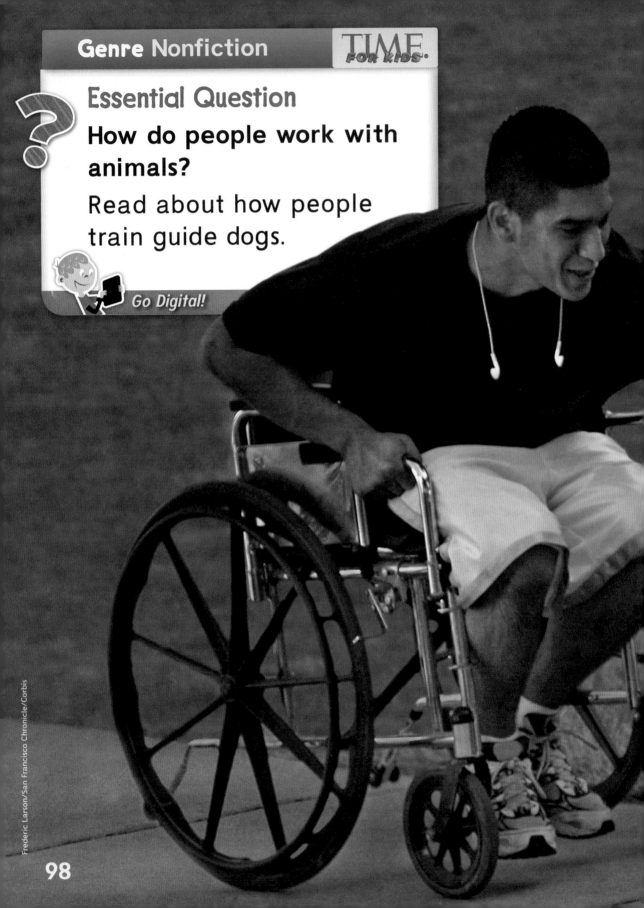

Essential Question

How do people work with animals?

Read about how people train guide dogs.

Go Digital!

From Puppy to Guide Dog

Most dogs are pets. But some dogs help people. What is the key to making a dog a good helping dog?

A Buddy-to-Be

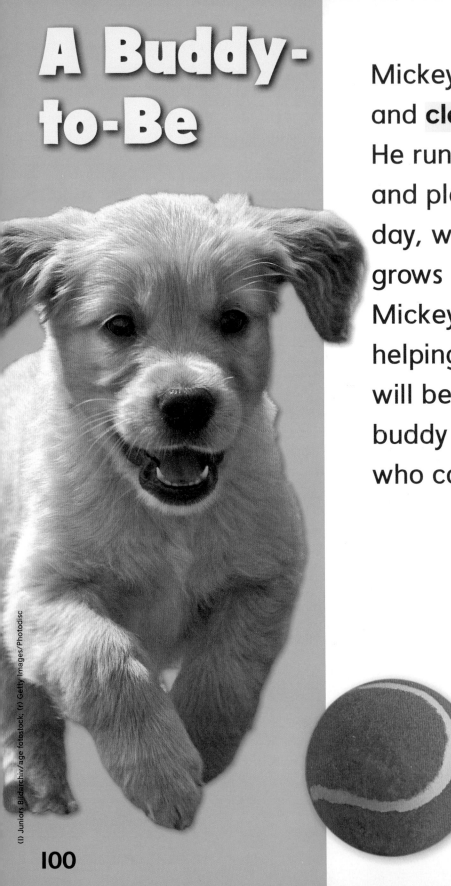

Mickey is a cute and **clever** puppy. He runs, jumps, and plays. One day, when he grows up a bit, Mickey will be a helping dog. He will be a daily buddy to a person who cannot see.

Helping dogs are called guide dogs. To be a guide dog, a puppy must be bright. It cannot be lazy or fussy. The puppy will need to learn many skills. A new home is **found** for the puppy when it is eight weeks old.

Fact

Most guide dogs are Labrador retrievers. They are very intelligent and easy to train.

▼ Guide dogs can be big or tiny.

Ryan McVay/Photolibrary

A Family of Trainers

A puppy like Mickey stays with a family for at least one year. The family plays with it and feeds it. They help the puppy stay healthy and teach the puppy a lot.

▲ Each puppy has checkups at the vet.

Fact

10,000 people in the U.S. and Canada use guide dogs.

Jim Craigmyle/Comet/Corbis

Each puppy learns how to act nicely with people and with other animals. The family gets the dog used to a lot of tasks and settings. Puppies may visit many kinds of places in the city. They go to homes and shops.

▲ This dog watches its favorite team.

▼ Every dog must be trained by itself.

Learning New Tasks

As time goes by, the dogs are trained how to go across the street. The dog stays right **near** the trainer. It learns to stop at a red **signal**. This will help the dog safely lead a person who cannot see the traffic.

Fact

Guide dogs are allowed in restaurants, stores, school—any place a person can go.

▲ This guide dog learns to cross a street.

Some guide dogs can be trained to help a man or a **woman** who cannot move or walk. He or she might need help with a lot of **hard** tasks both inside and outside the home.

A dog can be trained to get an elevator and to reach objects.

Eyes and Ears

Some dogs are trained to help people who cannot hear. If the dog hears a bell ringing or a yell, it **would** lightly tug or poke the person with its nose.

A dog can be taught to alert its owner to sounds.

Fact

Guide dogs should not be bothered while working.

Yan Sheng/CNImaging/Newscom

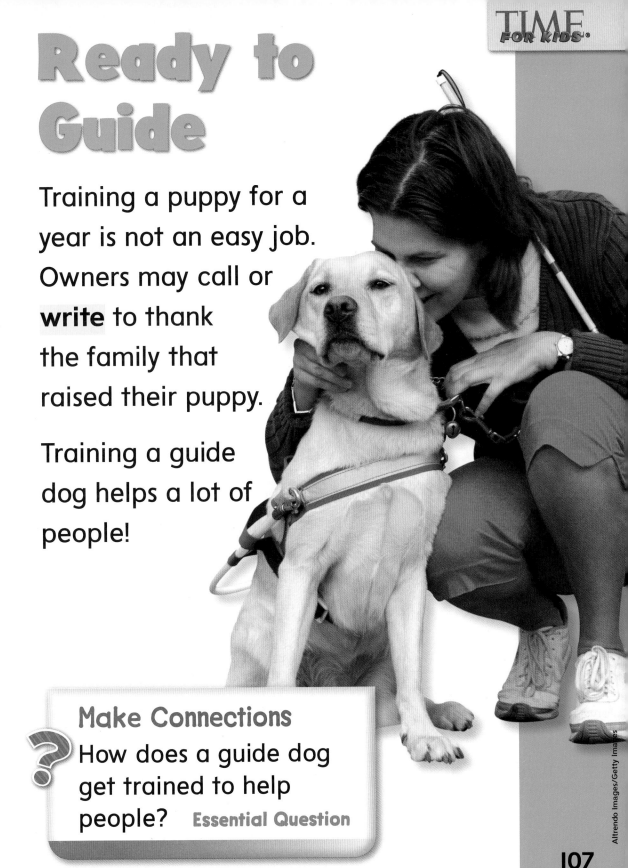

Ready to Guide

Training a puppy for a year is not an easy job. Owners may call or **write** to thank the family that raised their puppy.

Training a guide dog helps a lot of people!

Make Connections

? How does a guide dog get trained to help people? **Essential Question**

Altrendo Images/Getty Images

Sequence

Authors often give information in **sequence**, or time order.

 Find Text Evidence

Find one of the first things that happens to a guide dog puppy.

page 101

Helping dogs are called guide dogs. To be a guide dog, a puppy must be bright. It cannot be lazy or fussy. The puppy will need to learn many skills. A new home is **found** for the puppy when it is eight weeks old.

Ryan McVay/Photolibrary

First

An eight-week-old puppy leaves its mother.

Next

It lives with a training family for one year.

Then

The puppy learns harder tasks. It becomes a good guide dog.

Last

The guide dog is given to a needy person.

Your Turn

COLLABORATE

Talk about the sequence of a guide dog's life in "From Puppy to Guide Dog."

Go Digital! *Use the interactive graphic organizer*

From Puppy to **Guide Dog**

Pages 98–107

Write About the Text

Hassan

Time-Order Words

I used the word <u>after</u> to tell when Mickey will need to do different things.

I answered the question: **Why does the family get Mickey used to a lot of tasks and settings?**

Student Model: *Informative Text*

The family needs to get Mickey ready to be a guide dog. After Mickey is trained, he will do a lot of different things. Mickey might go to a big city. Mickey cannot be afraid. He has to go into shops and restaurants.

A guide dog must act calmly and not bark. The family trains Mickey to be around people. The family takes him to games. Later, Mickey will know how to act in a crowd.

Concluding Statement
I wrapped up my answer.

Grammar
Later is an **adverb** that tells when.

Your Turn

Based on pages 104–106, what should a guide dog do well after being trained? Use text evidence.

Go Digital!
Write your response online.
Use your editing checklist.

Figure It Out

The **Big** Idea

How can we make sense of the world around us?

My Shadow

I have a little shadow that goes in
and out with me,

And what can be the use of
him is more than I can see.

He is very, very like me from
the heels up to the head;

And I see him jump before me,
when I jump into my bed.

—by Robert Louis Stevenson

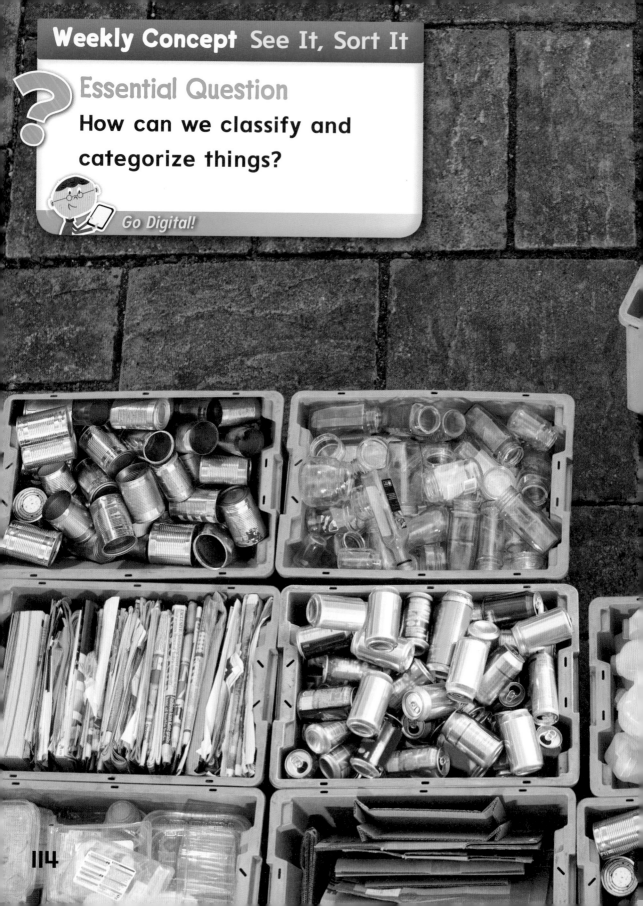

Essential Question

How can we classify and categorize things?

Go Digital!

Mix and Match

COLLABORATE

Talk About It

How is this girl sorting things?

four

A sheep has **four** legs.

large

We picked a **large** pumpkin.

none

None of the dogs has spots.

only

This goat has **only** one kid.

put

We **put** the best peaches in the box.

round

A tractor has big **round** wheels.

trouble

A goat can get into **trouble**!

whole

The **whole** barn is painted red.

COLLABORATE

Your Turn

Read the sentence for each word. Then make up another sentence.

Go Digital! *Use the online visual glossary*

<u>ar</u>

The letters <u>ar</u> can make the sounds you hear in the middle of **b<u>ar</u>n**.

p<u>ar</u>t	f<u>ar</u>m	p<u>ar</u>k
l<u>ar</u>ge	m<u>ar</u>ching	sm<u>ar</u>t
sh<u>ar</u>p	h<u>ar</u>d	st<u>ar</u>ted
rest<u>ar</u>t	backy<u>ar</u>d	<u>ar</u>tist

Jack Hughes

Marge has a large farm with a red barn.

She parks her car in the yard.

Your Turn

Look for these words with ar in "A Barn
Full of Hats."

barn	farm	smart
marched	yarn	apart
Clark	large	barnyard

Essential Question

How can we classify and categorize things?

Read about how some farm animals sort hats.

 Go Digital!

Jack Hughes

120

A Barn Full of Hats

One day, **four** farm animals found a box in the barn. They opened it up.

What was inside? Hats, hats, and more hats!

"Look at all those hats! Who wants one?" asked Hen.

"I do!" cried Horse. "It's smart to wear a hat. A hat will keep the sun out of my eyes."

Hen stuck her head in the box. She pulled out a flat, **round** hat. "Try this hat," Hen told Horse.

"No, that hat is too flat," said Horse.

"A flat hat makes a good nest!" clucked Hen. So she took the hat and she marched away.

Pig pushed his head in the box. He pulled out a bright red hat. **"Put** on this hat," Pig told Horse.

"No, that hat is too red," said Horse.

"A red hat looks fine!" grunted Pig. So he put on the hat and he marched away.

Cat poked her head in the box.
She pulled out a thick yarn hat.
"Try this hat!" Cat told Horse.

"No, that hat is too thick," said Horse.

126

"Thick yarn is nice," said Cat. "I will take the **whole** hat apart, so I can play with the yarn." She dragged the hat away.

"So many hats, but **none** for me!" sighed Horse.

Just then, Farmer Clark came into the barn. His hat was **large** and floppy.

"If **only** I had that hat!" said Horse. "That hat will shade my eyes!"

Horse grabbed the hat in his teeth!

Farmer Clark laughed. He put the hat on Horse. It stayed on with no **trouble**. "It fits well," Farmer Clark said.

Horse trotted to the barnyard. Clip, clop! He held his head high. "Yes, this is the hat for me!" said Horse.

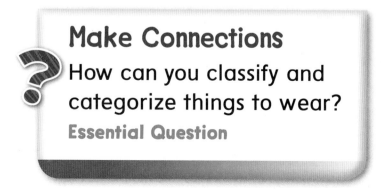

Make Connections

How can you classify and categorize things to wear?

Essential Question

Point of View

Point of view is the way that a story character thinks or feels.

What a character says helps you understand his or her point of view.

 Find Text Evidence

Find the point of view of one of the story characters.

page 123

"Look at all those hats! Who wants one?" asked Hen.

"I do!" cried Horse. "It's smart to wear a hat. A hat will keep the sun out of my eyes."

Jack Hughes

130

Character	Clue	Point of View
Horse	Thinks it's smart to wear a hat.	Wants something to shade his eyes from the sun.
Hen	Takes the hat to use as a nest.	Wants to find good materials for her nest.
Cat	Likes the hat made of thick yarn.	Wants something to play with.

Your Turn

COLLABORATE

Talk about the different points of view in "A Barn Full of Hats."

Go Digital! Use the interactive graphic organizer

Write About the Text

Pages 120-129

James

I answered the question: **Do you think Horse could have picked any of the other hats? Why or why not?**

Student Model: *Opinion*

I do not think that Horse could have picked a different hat. Horse did not like the other hats. Horse said the flat hat was too flat. The red hat was too red. The yarn hat was too thick.

Complete Sentences
I used complete sentences to tell my opinion.

Describing Details
I used details from the story to tell about each hat.

Horse picked Farmer Clark's hat because it was large and floppy. It kept the sun from Horse's eyes. It fit Horse perfectly! Horse chose the only hat for him.

Grammar

The word <u>because</u> is a **conjunction.** It joins two sentences.

Your Turn

COLLABORATE

Did each of the animals choose the right hat? Why or why not? Use text evidence to support your answer.

Go Digital!
Write your response online.
Use your editing checklist.

133

Weekly Concept Up in the Sky

Essential Question

What can you see in the sky?

Go Digital!

Talk About It

What does this girl
see in the night sky?

(bkgd)StockTrek/Photodisc/Getty Images; (r)Image Source/Getty Images

134

Night
and Day

another

Will **another** cloud cover the sun?

climb

That cat can **climb** a tree quickly.

full

There is a **full** moon out tonight.

great

It is a **great** day for a picnic!

poor

My **poor** dog got wet in the rain.

through

Can you see the man **through** the fog?

leaped

The frog **leaped** into the lake.

stretched

The rainbow **stretched** out across the sky.

Your Turn

COLLABORATE

Read the sentence for each word. Then make up another sentence.

Go Digital! *Use the online visual glossary*

er, ir, ur, or

The letters er, ir, ur, and or can make the sounds you hear in the middle of **term**, **bird**, **curl**, and **worm**.

girl	dirt	hurt
her	worked	third
turns	verb	first
shirt	word	nurse

Lisa Hunt

Did that burst of thunder wake Herb?

Herb woke up first and turned over.

Your Turn

COLLABORATE

Look for these words with er, ir, ur, and or in "A Bird Named Fern."

bird	Fern	world
herself	her	surprised
better	turned	first

Essential Question

What can you see in the sky?

Read how a bird named Fern learns about clouds.

Go Digital!

Lisa Hunt

A Bird Named Fern

Little Fern was always **full** of questions! She wanted to know about everything in the world.

Lisa Hunt

142

One day, Fern saw something up in the sky.

"What is that big, white boat doing in the sky?" she asked herself. "I want to find out."

"It would be **great** to ride on that big white boat," Fern said. So she **stretched** her wings and took off.

144

Fern's wings helped her **climb** up, up, up.

But when she got close to the boat, she was surprised. The boat looked like a fluffy bed!

145

Fern was sleepy and wanted to rest. So she **leaped** on the bed. But she fell right **through** it!

"I see **another** bed," said Fern. "I will try to land on that one."

But the same thing happened again!

"I'd better go home," cried Fern. "Maybe Mom and Dad can explain this."

So Fern began to fly home. As she did, the beds turned dark gray. Then it started to rain. **Poor** Fern was soaked when she got home.

"Where were you?" asked Mom and Dad.

Fern told them all about her trip.

"First we will dry you off," said Mom.

"Then we will teach you about clouds," added Dad.

And that is what they did!

Make Connections

? What did the clouds look like to Fern? **Essential Question**

Cause and Effect

A **cause** is what makes something happen in a story.

An **effect** is the event that happens.

To figure out cause and effect, ask yourself: What happened? Why did it happen?

 Find Text Evidence

Find a cause and its effect in the story.

page 144

"It would be **great** to ride on that big white boat," Fern said. So she **stretched** her wings and took off.

150

Cause		Effect

Fern wanted to ride on the big white boat.		Fern stretched her wings and took off.
The boat looked like a fluffy bed up close.		Fern was surprised.
It started to rain.		Fern got soaked.

Your Turn

Talk about the cause and effect of story events in "A Bird Named Fern."

Go Digital! *Use the interactive graphic organizer*

Write About the Text

Pages 140-149

Carla

I answered the question: **Why couldn't Fern ride on the boat in the sky or lie on the beds? How do you know?**

Student Model: *Informative Text*

Describing Words

I used the word <u>fluffy</u> to describe the beds.

Fern couldn't ride on the boat because it was a cloud.

Fern could not lie on the fluffy beds because they were also clouds. When Fern tried to lie on the clouds she fell through them.

Grammar

<u>White</u> and <u>puffy</u> are **adjectives** that describe the clouds.

I know they were clouds because the ship and beds look like clouds in the pictures. They are white, puffy, and in the sky.

At the end, Fern's dad said he would teach her about clouds. This is a clue that the bed and boat are clouds.

Clues

I used what Fern's dad said as a clue about the clouds.

Your Turn

How does the author show that Fern is curious? Use text evidence to support your answer.

Go Digital!
Write your response online.
Use your editing checklist.

Essential Question

What inventions do you know about?

Go Digital!

Talk About It

How do you use this invention?

A New Idea

began

He **began** to build a robot.

better

Let's invent a **better** umbrella!

guess

Can you **guess** what this does?

learn

You can **learn** how to sign just like me!

right

This clock tells the **right** time.

sure

She makes **sure** you are well.

idea

New bulbs are a good **idea**!

unusual

This new bike is **unusual**.

Your Turn

COLLABORATE

Read the sentence for each word. Then make up another sentence.

Go Digital! *Use the online visual glossary*

or, oar, ore

The letters or, oar, and ore can make the sounds you hear at the end of **for**, **roar**, and **more**.

oar	born	tore
shorter	store	board
roaring	wore	form
sports	north	before

Morty built a better board for the shore.

Are there some more at the sports store?

Your Turn

Look for these words with or, oar, and ore in "The Story of a Robot Inventor."

story	born	sorts	forms	more
short	for	sports	soar	

159

Essential Question
What inventions do you know about?

Read about someone who invents robots.

Go Digital!

The Story of a Robot Inventor

Big Ideas

Meet Tomotaka Takahashi. He invents **unusual** robots. How did he get started?

Mr. Takahashi was born in Japan in 1975. As a child, he played with blocks. He used his imagination to make all sorts of forms and shapes.

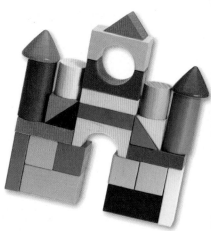

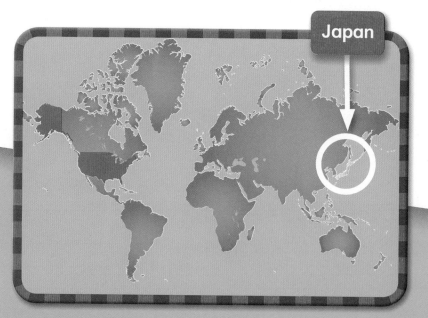

Japan

Later, he read comic books about a robot named Astro Boy. The robot looked like a real child. Takahashi wanted to make robots just like it.

Finding Out About Robots

In 1999, Takahashi **began** to study robots. He took classes to **learn** how they move. The robots bent their legs when they walked. It did not look **right** to Takahashi. People did not walk that way.

Then Takahashi had an **idea**. He made a **better** robot. It did not bend its legs when it walked. It moved more like a person.

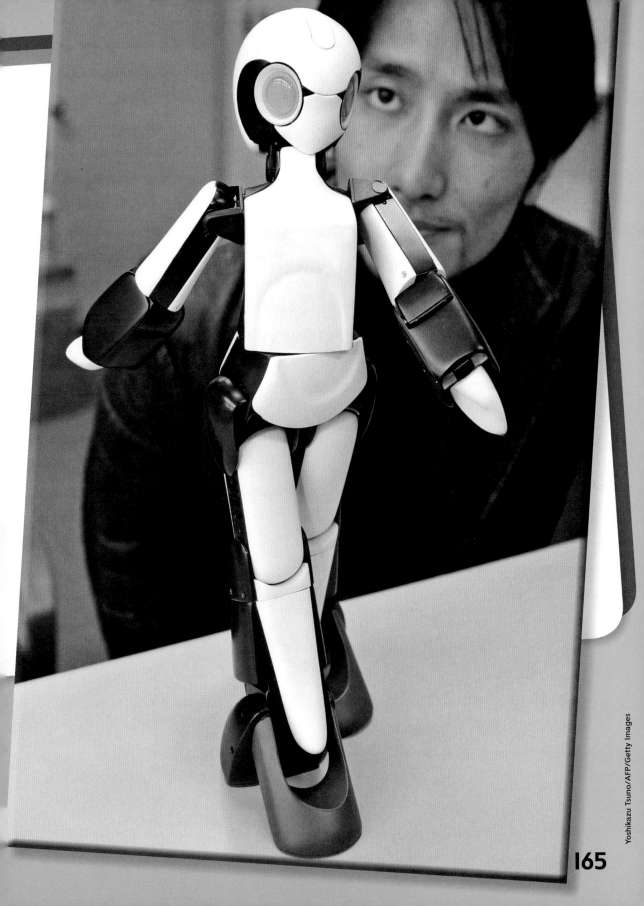

Making Better Robots

In 2003, Takahashi started his own company. He made many robots. A short robot climbed up a cliff with a rope. A bigger robot lifted a car with its arms. Another robot rode a bike for 24 hours.

Takahashi began to put his robots in contests. He made three robots for a sports race in Hawaii in 2011. The first robot had to swim. The second robot had to ride a bike. The third robot had to run. The robots had to do these tasks for a week!

Toru Yamanaka/AFP/Getty Images

For the race, there were many problems to solve. Takahashi made the swimming robot waterproof. He gave it arms like fins to help it swim faster. Another robot was able to ride its bike for 100 miles without breaking. The third robot ran for 26 miles!

What will Takahashi invent next? Will his robots fly and soar like Astro Boy? Will they be his finest? We can only **guess**. We must wait and see.

Tomotaka Takahashi is **sure** of one thing. His robots will do more and more!

Make Connections

What kind of robot would you like to invent? **Essential Question**

Kyodo via AP Images

Problem and Solution

A **problem** is something that a person wants to do, change, or find out. The way the person solves the problem is the **solution**.

Find Text Evidence

Find one of the problems that Mr. Takahashi faced when building robots for the race.

page 167

Takahashi began to put his robots in contests. He made three robots for a sports race in Hawaii in 2011. The first robot had to swim. The second robot had to ride a bike. The third robot had to run. The robots had to do these tasks for a week!

Problem

Takahashi wanted to put a robot in a race where it had to swim.

Steps to Solution

He built a waterproof robot with arms like fins.

Solution

Takahashi built his robot in a way that it could swim.

COLLABORATE

Your Turn

Talk about the problems the inventor faced in "The Story of a Robot Inventor" and how he solved them.

Go Digital! *Use the interactive graphic organizer*

The Story of a
Robot Inventor

Write About the Text

Pages 160–169

Emily

I responded to the prompt: **Look at pages 162–165. What can you tell about what makes a good inventor?**

Student Model: *Informative Text*

Facts
I supplied some facts about the topic from the selection.

Tomotaka Takahashi is a good inventor. Good inventors like to play and make new things. They get ideas from reading. Takahashi got ideas about making robots by reading comic books. Good inventors think about details and how to make them better.

Time-Order Words

I used <u>first</u> and <u>next</u> to tell the order in which Takahashi made a better robot.

Grammar

The **comparative adjective** <u>older</u> is used correctly.

First, Takahashi looked at how older robots move. He saw that robots did not move their legs like people. Next, Takahashi made a robot that moved more like a person. The robot did not bend its legs.

COLLABORATE

Your Turn

Look at pages 166–169. What can you tell about what makes a good inventor from these pages? Include text evidence to support your answer.

Go Digital!
Write your response online.
Use your editing checklist.

Essential Question

What sounds can you hear?
How are they made?

Go Digital!

Listen Up!

Talk About It

How are these children making sounds?

175

color

This bird is a
bright **color**.

early

Early morning
can be very quiet.

instead

I try to whisper
instead of shouting.

nothing

There is **nothing**
in that can.

oh

Oh, our marching band
has a great sound!

thought

He **thought** the jet was much too loud.

scrambled

Goats **scrambled** up the rocks.

suddenly

The sky **suddenly** lit up brightly!

(t to b, l to r) Tim Laman/National Geographic/Getty Images; Ingram Publishing/SuperStock; Nancy R. Cohen/Photodisc/Getty Images; Eco Images/Universal Images Group/Getty Images; Gary Conner/Photolibrary/Getty Images; Brand X Pictures/PunchStock; Bruce & Jan Lichtenberger/SuperStock; NOAA Photo Library, NOAA Central Library: OAR/ERL/National Severe Storms Laboratory (NSSL)

COLLABORATE

Your Turn

Read the sentence for each word. Then make up another sentence.

Go Digital! Use the online visual glossary

<u>ou</u>, <u>ow</u>

> The letters <u>ou</u> and <u>ow</u> can make the sound you hear in the middle of **found** and **down**.

loud	now	ground
brown	shouted	growling
frowned	cloud	pound
mouse	around	towel

We found a brown puppy in town.

It does not growl or make loud sounds!

Your Turn

COLLABORATE

Look for these words with ou and ow in "Now, What's That Sound?"

now	sound	out	house
bouncing	shouted	wow	
crown	down	sounds	

Genre Realistic Fiction

Essential Question

What sounds can you hear?
How are they made?

Read about two children
who hunt for a sound.

Go Digital!

Now, What's That Sound?

Tap-tap-tap. Rat-a-tat-tat.

"What's that sound?" asked Gilbert. "It started **early** this morning. I **thought** it might stop, but it hasn't!"

"Let's check out the garage," said Marta. "I think Dad is making the sound."

Tap-tap-tap
Rat-a-tat-tat

Zing
Zing
Zing

Dad was in the garage cutting a board with his saw.

Zing, zing, zing.

"This is not the sound," said Gilbert. "This sound is smoother."

"Let's find Gramps," said Marta. "He might be making the sound."

They quickly ran to the back of the house to find Gramps.

Pablo Bernasconi

Gramps was sweeping the deck with a broom.

Swish, swish, swish.

"No, this is not the sound," said Gilbert. "This sound is much softer."

Swish

Swish

Swish

"Let's find Ana **instead**," said Marta. "Maybe she's making the sound."

They found Ana in the driveway. Ana was bouncing a ball.

Bam. . . bam . . . bam.

Pablo Bernasconi

"No, this is not the sound," said Gilbert. "This sound is slower."

"This is hopeless!" sighed Marta.

Tap-tap-tap. Rat-a-tat-tat.

"There it is again," said Gilbert. He looked up at the tallest tree. **Suddenly**, he shouted. "**Oh**, wow! It's a bird!"

"Look at the **color** on its head," cried Marta. "It's red, like a red crown."

The bird **scrambled** up and down the tree.

Tap-tap-tap. Rat-a-tat-tat.

Tap-tap-tap!
Rat-a-tat-tat!

"It's a woodpecker pecking for bugs," said Gilbert.

"Yes," said Marta. "And **nothing** else sounds like it!"

Tap-tap-tap! Rat-a-tat-tat!

Make Connections

How are the sounds around you made? **Essential Question**

Problem and Solution

A **problem** is something characters want to do, change, or find out. The way the problem is solved is the **solution**.

🔍 Find Text Evidence

Find the problem that the story characters need to solve.

page 182

Tap-tap-tap. Rat-a-tat-tat.

"What's that sound?" asked Gilbert. "It started **early** this morning. I **thought** it might stop, but it hasn't!"

"Let's check out the garage," said Marta. "I think Dad is making the sound."

Pablo Bernasconi

Problem

Gilbert and Marta hear a new sound.

Steps to Solution

Check if Dad is making the sound.

Check if Gramps is making the sound.

Check if Ana is making the sound.

Solution

Gilbert and Marta discover that the sound is a woodpecker tapping on a tree.

COLLABORATE

Your Turn

Talk about the problem and solution in "Now, What's That Sound?"

Go Digital! Use the interactive graphic organizer

Write About the Text

Pages 180-189

Jacob

I responded to the prompt: **Rewrite pages 188-189. Make the source of the sound different.**

Student Model: *Narrative Text*

"There is that sound again," Gilbert said to Marta.

"I know that sound," said Marta.

Complete Sentences
I wrote in complete sentences to express my ideas.

They walked by a small house. A little girl was sitting on the porch. She was playing a red drum using two sticks. She made the sound.

Tap-tap-tap. Rat-a-tat-tat.

Tap-tap-tap
Rat-a-tat-tat

Grammar
The **article** <u>a</u> is used correctly.

Concluding Sentence
I added the last sentence to help organize my writing.

"You are a good drummer,"
Gilbert said to the little girl.

"Thanks!" the little girl said.
"I want to play in a band one day."

"We found the sound!"
said Marta.

Your Turn

Write a detective story about a sound. Use the same story structure as "Now, What's That Sound?"

Go Digital!
Write your response online.
Use your editing checklist.

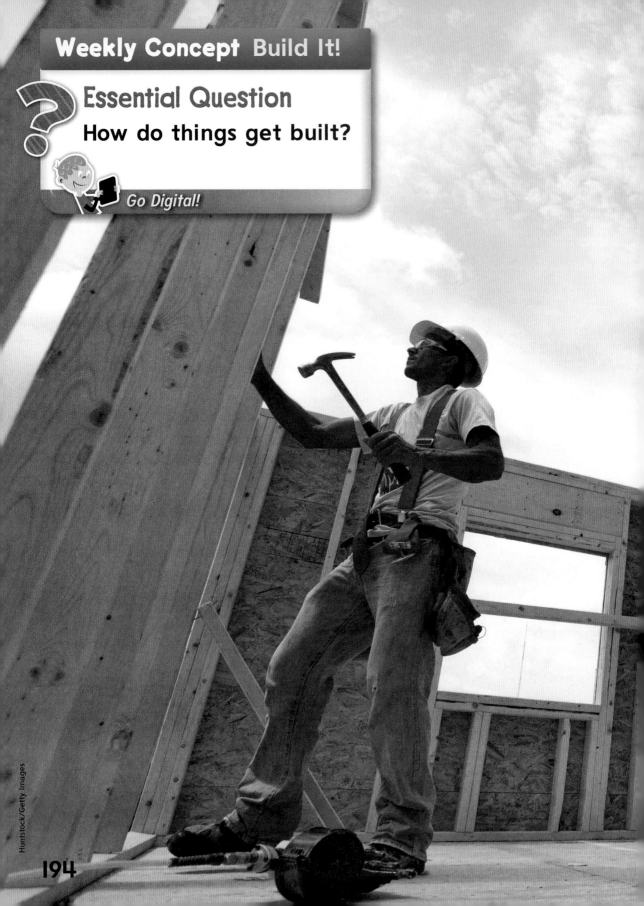

Essential Question

How do things get built?

Go Digital!

Up It Goes!

Talk About It

What is this carpenter building?
How is he doing it?

195

above

The cranes are **above** the building.

build

They will **build** some houses.

fall

It is strong and will not **fall**.

knew

She **knew** how to make a good model.

money

I put my **money** in a new bank.

toward

We walked **toward** the water.

balance

The worker can **balance** up high.

section

This **section** is not finished yet.

(t to b, l to r) Stockbyte/Getty Images; Panorama Media/age fotostock; Royalty-Free/Corbis; Radius/SuperStock; Hill Street Studios/Blend Images/SuperStock; IT Stock/PunchStock; Bruce Edwards/America 24-7/Getty Images; Ryan McVay/Photodisc/Getty Images

Your Turn

COLLABORATE

Read the sentence for each word. Then make up another sentence.

Go Digital! *Use the online visual glossary*

oy, oi

The letters oy and oi can make the sound you hear in the middle of **toys** and **point**.

oil	joined	boiling
boy	hoist	enjoy
moist	employ	choice
annoys	noise	destroy

Let's av<u>oi</u>d ann<u>oy</u>ing this b<u>oy</u>.

He does not enj<u>oy</u> the n<u>oi</u>se!

Your Turn

Look for these words with <u>oy</u> and <u>oi</u> in "The Joy of a Ship."

j<u>oy</u>	empl<u>oy</u>s	h<u>oi</u>st
av<u>oi</u>d	b<u>oi</u>ls	j<u>oi</u>ns
j<u>oi</u>nts	p<u>oi</u>nt	m<u>oi</u>st

Essential Question

How do things get built?

Read about building a ship.

Go Digital!

Engel & Gielen/VISUM/The Image Works

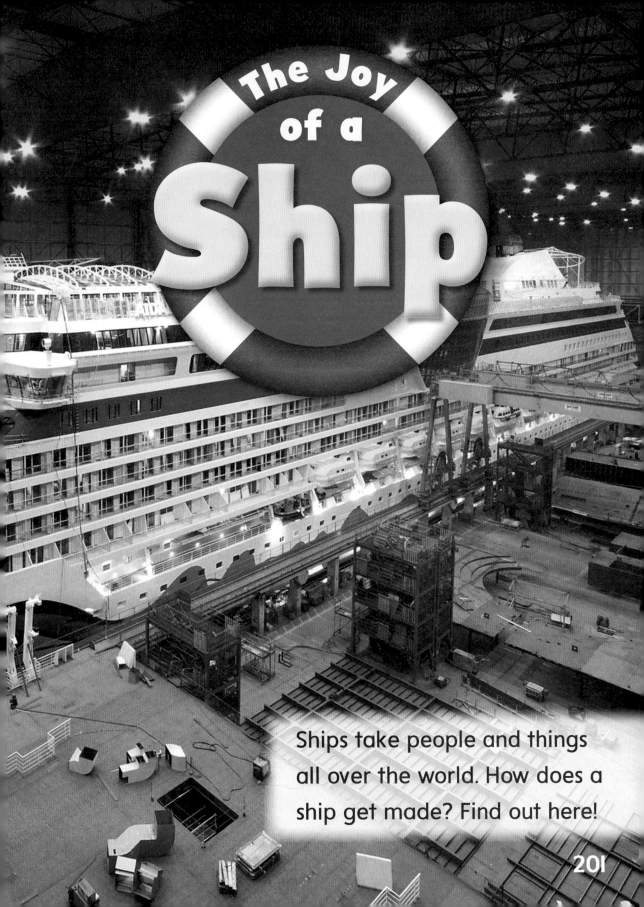

The Joy of a Ship

Ships take people and things all over the world. How does a ship get made? Find out here!

What is needed to **build** a ship? Making ships employs many workers. This task uses lots of tools and parts as well. Let's see how a ship is made, step by step.

These people study the plans for the ship. There are many things to do!

Frame It!

First, workers build a frame. The ship frame can **balance** on blocks up **above** a dock. Huge cranes hoist the big parts in place so they do not **fall**. Workers must avoid being bumped by these big pieces of steel.

Some huge gantry cranes can lift 1,500 tons as high as 230 feet in the air.

Sheets of Steel

First, two kinds of metal are melted into steel. It boils! Hot steel flows into flat metal sheets and molds. When steel gets cold, it gets hard. The steel sheets are then ready for making a ship.

Stand back! The steel is very hot!

A worker joins each steel **section** by heating the edges, called joints. Most workers put on gloves and a helmet to protect their hands and head.

enviromantic/Vetta/Getty Images

Check It, Paint It

Workers check all the joints. Then they point out leaks and fix them. If a joint leaks, the inside of this ship will be moist with water. It might even sink!

Fritz Hoffmann/In Pictures/Corbis

Then, the ship is painted, and this job is done! It gleams in the sun. The workers **knew** it would look nice! People will pay a lot of **money** to ride on this ship.

Markus Hibbeler/AFP/Getty Images

Out to Sea!

The people on the dock point with joy as the new ship begins the first trip! Those on the ship wave as it glides **toward** the open sea.

Did you know?

There are many kinds of ships on the sea.

Ice Breaker Ship ▼

Aircraft Carrier ▼

Cargo Ship ▼

Make Connections

What steps in ship building are risky? **Essential Question**

(bl) Purestock/SuperStock; (tr) USCG photo by Patrick Kelley; (br) BananaStock/JupiterImages

Cause and Effect

A **cause** is how or why something happens.
An **effect** is what happens.

Find Text Evidence

Find what causes hot steel to get hard.

page 204

First, two kinds of metal are melted into steel. It boils! Hot steel flows into flat metal sheets and molds. When steel gets cold, it gets hard. The steel sheets are then ready for making a ship.

Getty Images

Cause		Effect
Hot steel gets cold.		The steel gets hard.
A worker wears a helmet and gloves.		The worker's head and hands are safe.
A joint leaks on a ship.		The ship gets moist with water. It might sink.

COLLABORATE

Your Turn

Talk about what happens in "The Joy of a Ship" and how or why it happens.

Go Digital! Use the interactive graphic organizer

Write About the Text

Pages 200–209

Michael

I answered the question: **What do you think is the most important step in building a ship? Why?**

Student Model: *Opinion*

Topic
I named the selection and stated the topic.

Reasons
I included a reason for my opinion.

After reading "The Joy of a Ship," I think the most important step in building a ship is building a frame. The ship needs a strong frame to be safe.

First, workers study a plan. Then, they make the frame.

Next, workers add steel sheets
to the frame. The sheets form
the sides of the ship.

I think the frame is the most
important step because
if the frame is not right,
the sides might leak.

Grammar

**The word
of is a
preposition.**

COLLABORATE

Your Turn

What do you think is
the least important
step in building a ship?
Why? Use text evidence
to support your answer.

Go Digital!
Write your response online.
Use your editing checklist.

213

Unit 6
Together We Can!

Together

Together is better,
    Whatever we do,

You get so much more done,
    When someone helps you.

If someone is lonely,
    And not having fun,
Just ask them to play;

    Two is better than one.

And books sound much better,
    When shared with a friend,

Together is better,
    Beginning to end.

—by Constance A. Kareme

The Big Idea

How does teamwork help us?

215

Essential Question

How can we work together to make our lives better?

Go Digital!

Make It Happen!

Talk About It

What are these people working on together?

217

answer

I know the **answer** to that question!

brought

We all **brought** food for the picnic.

busy

The bees are **busy** making honey.

door

Grandpa met us at the **door**.

enough

Are there **enough** seats for all?

eyes

Our **eyes** and ears help us learn.

demand

People can **demand** fair pay.

emergency

A fire is one kind of **emergency**.

Your Turn

COLLABORATE

Read the sentence for each word. Then make up another sentence.

Go Digital! Use the online visual glossary

oo, u, u_e, ew, ue, ui, ou

The letters oo, u, u_e, ew, ue, ui, and ou can make the sound you hear in the middle of **cool**, **truth**, **flute**, **news**, **clues**, **suit**, and **soup**.

moon	June	student
flew	true	fruit
you	room	July
rude	group	chewing

Lucy and a group of friends sat by the pool.

Lucy, Sue, and Drew ate fruit.

Your Turn

Look for these words with oo, u, u_e, ew, ue, ui, and ou in "Super Tools."

super	tools	few	new
cool	Lucy	used	useless
rude	soon	juice	drew
blue	you	room	useful

Essential Question

How can we work together to make our lives better?

Read about how a girl's forgotten writing tools work together to become useful again.

Go Digital!

Gynux

Super Tools

A few weeks ago, Lucy's mom and dad **brought** a new computer home. "This is so cool!" exclaimed Lucy.
Lucy used the computer all the time.

But not everyone was happy about the new computer.

Dear Gram,
When will
you visit us ?

Lucy didn't know it, but her writing tools felt sad and useless. One day while she was at school, they had an **emergency** meeting.

"Lucy hasn't used us in weeks!" cried the markers. "Can we **demand** to be used?" asked the crayons. "No, that would be rude. But, we can remind her how great we are," said the pencils. "Yes!" they all agreed. "Let's remind her."

After school, as soon as Lucy came through the **door**, she grabbed a glass of juice and went right to her computer. She had to write a report about birds.

The writing tools watched and waited. When Lucy was done, she printed her report.

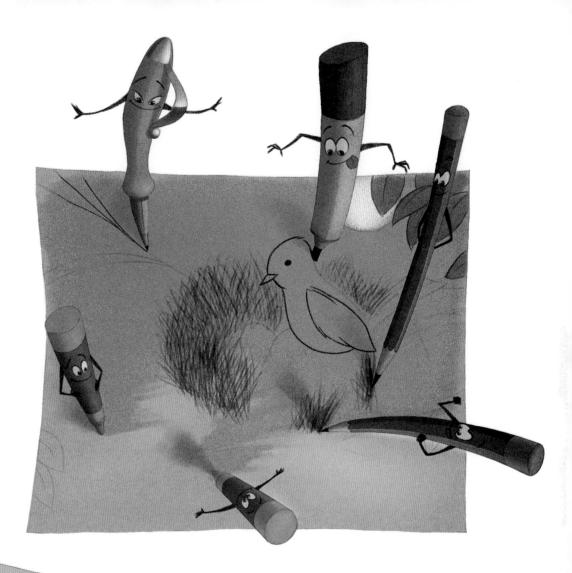

That night the writing tools got **busy**. They worked together to make a picture for Lucy.

The pencils made a sketch. The markers drew the birds in the tree. The crayons drew the sun in a blue sky. The picture was good **enough** to frame.

The next day was Saturday. Lucy woke up
late. Then she went to get her report. Lucy
gasped. She couldn't believe her **eyes**!
"Who drew this great picture?" she asked.

Gynux

"Did you draw this?" Lucy asked Mom and Dad.
"You know the **answer** to that!" they laughed.
"Stop joking! YOU drew that great picture."

That made Lucy think she wished she had drawn it. "It is fun to draw," she said.

Lucy hung the picture in her room. Then she took out her pencils, crayons, and markers. "I'll draw my own picture for my report," she said.

Lucy and her pencils, crayons, and markers worked together. They drew a super picture.

From that day on, Lucy kept drawing. And the writing tools felt happy and useful!

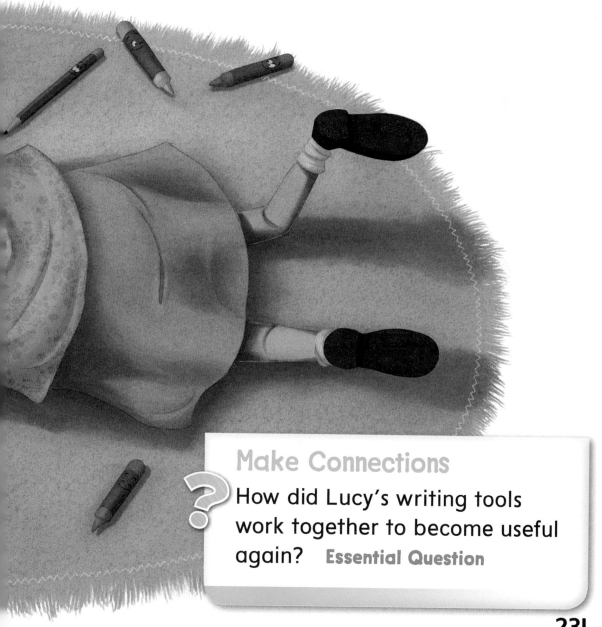

Make Connections

How did Lucy's writing tools work together to become useful again? **Essential Question**

Theme

The **theme** is the big idea or message of a story.

 Find Text Evidence

Find clues that help you understand the theme.

page 227

That night the writing tools got **busy**. They worked together to make a picture for Lucy.

The pencils made a sketch. The markers drew the birds in the tree. The crayons drew the sun in a blue sky. The picture was good **enough** to frame.

Clue

The pencils made a sketch.

Clue

The markers drew the birds in the tree.

Clue

The crayons drew the sun in a blue sky.

Theme

The writing tools worked together to make their lives better.

COLLABORATE

Your Turn

Talk about the theme of "Super Tools."

Go Digital! Use the interactive graphic organizer

Write About the Text

Pages 222–231

Billy

I responded to the prompt: **Write a letter from the computer to the tools. Tell how Lucy can use all of them.**

Student Model: *Narrative*

Dear Writing Tools,

Vary Sentence Length
Short and long sentences make my letter interesting.

Lucy is excited to use me. I am new, and she thinks I'm cool! She can use me to type a letter to Gran.

I am great for reports, too. She can use me to type it up and print it out.

Details
I included details from the story.

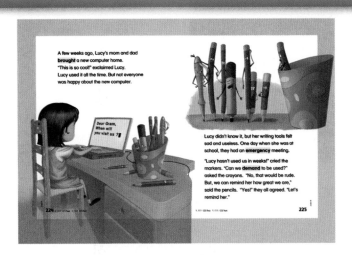

A few weeks ago, Lucy's mom and dad **brought** a new computer home. "This is so cool!" exclaimed Lucy. Lucy used it all the time. But not everyone was happy about the new computer.

Dear Gram, When will you visit us?

Lucy didn't know it, but her writing tools felt sad and useless. One day when she was at school, they had an **emergency** meeting.

"Lucy hasn't used us in weeks!" cried the markers. "Can we **demand** to be used?" asked the crayons. "No, that would be rude. But, we can remind her how great we are," said the pencils. "Yes!" they all agreed. "Let's remind her."

224   225

Grammar

<u>She</u> is a **pronoun.**

She can add to the report by drawing a beautiful picture. She needs you for that!

I am new, but I think Lucy will use all of us from now on. We can all work together!

Your pal,
Your Computer

Your Turn

COLLABORATE

Write a letter from the writing tools to Lucy explaining in words what they explained to her in their drawing.

Go Digital!
Write your response online.
Use your editing checklist.

235

Essential Question

Who helps you?

Go Digital!

My Helpers

COLLABORATE **Talk About It**

How does this girl get help from her coach?

237

brother

I like to read to
my **brother**.

father

My **father** shows
me how to swim.

friend

It's fun to have
a good **friend**!

love

My family and I
love each other.

mother

Pam's **mother** is
our soccer coach.

picture

I drew a **picture** for my teacher.

accept

Will you **accept** this gift?

often

We **often** go to the library.

Your Turn

COLLABORATE

Read the sentence for each word. Then make up another sentence.

Go Digital! Use the online visual glossary

<u>a</u>, <u>aw</u>, <u>au</u>, <u>augh</u>, <u>al</u>

The letters <u>a</u>, <u>aw</u>, <u>au</u>, <u>augh</u>, and <u>al</u> stand for the sound you hear in the middle of **ca<u>ll</u>s**, **f<u>aw</u>n**, **c<u>au</u>se**, **c<u>augh</u>t**, and **w<u>al</u>k**.

ball	talking	haul
saw	salt	taught
fault	smallest	yawn
also	pause	daughter

Last fall, I taught Paul how to draw.

He drew a tall tree using chalk.

Your Turn

COLLABORATE

Look for these words with a, aw, au, augh, and al in "All Kinds of Helpers."

all	also	baseball	ball
talks	taught	awful	because
caught	walk	always	talk

Essential Question

Who helps you?

Read about the people in your community who help you and the different ways they help.

Go Digital!

All Kinds of Helpers

Every day, people help us in many ways. To help means to give what is needed and useful. It also means to make things better. So helpers are the people who give us what we need and who make our lives better.

Who are some of the people who help us?

Families can be helpers. The people in a family **love** and **accept** us. They also help us in many ways.

A family can include a **mother** and a **father**. This boy also has a big **brother**. His brother **often** helps him with his homework. His mother and father help him learn about the world.

Teachers help you in many ways.
In school, a teacher helps you learn
how to read and write. A teacher
teaches you such subjects as math
and social studies. A teacher helps
you understand new ideas.

Sports coaches are helpers, too. The baseball coach in this **picture** is teaching his team how to hold the ball. He talks to them and shows them what to do. Who taught you how to play a sport?

Doctors and nurses help keep you healthy. You visit the doctor for a checkup or when you feel sick.

The girl in this picture feels awful because she caught a bad cold! But the doctor will help her get better.

Do you walk or take a bus to school? Either way, people help you get back and forth safely.

Other helpers keep you safe, too. Police officers and firefighters are always protecting you.

Some boys and girls need a grownup to talk to. Some groups match boys and girls with a grownup who will be their **friend**. What a good idea!

A special group called **Big Brothers Big Sisters** helps some children out.

There are many helpers around you. Families love you, and teachers help you learn. Doctors, nurses, and safety helpers keep you healthy and safe. Special groups help you in special ways. All of them give what is needed and useful.

Make Connections

Who are the people in your community that help you? How do they help? **Essential Question**

Author's Purpose

The **author's purpose** is the reason why an author writes a selection.

🔍 Find Text Evidence

Find a clue to help you understand the author's purpose.

page 251

There are many helpers around you. Families love you, and teachers help you learn. Doctors, nurses, and safety helpers keep you healthy and safe. Special groups help you in special ways. All of them give what is needed and useful.

Clue

Families love you, and teachers help you learn.

Clue

Doctors, nurses, and safety helpers keep you healthy and safe.

Author's Purpose

To let you know that there are many people helping you in many ways.

COLLABORATE

Your Turn

Talk about the author's purpose for writing "All Kinds of Helpers."

Go Digital! *Use the interactive graphic organizer*

Skip Nall/Corbis

Write About the Text

Pages 242–251

I responded to the prompt: **Pick one group from "All Kinds of Helpers" that has helped you and describe how.**

Farah

Student Model: *Informative Text*

My bus driver is someone who helps me get to and from school. Her name is Mrs. Johnson.

Mrs. Johnson is the best! I was nervous on the first day of school and she helped me. She told me where to get off the bus.

Topic
I wrote about someone in a group who has helped me.

Use Your Own Voice
I told how I feel about Mrs. Johnson.

Mrs. Johnson protects all the kids on her bus. Sometimes the bus is crowded. Mrs. Johnson tells everyone to sit down.

When we get off the bus, Mrs. Johnson tells us when it is time to cross the street. Mrs. Johnson helps keep me safe!

Grammar

<u>Her</u> is a **possessive pronoun.**

COLLABORATE

Your Turn

Write about a group of helpers in your community. Use "All Kinds of Helpers" as a model.

Go Digital!
Write your response online.
Use your editing checklist.

moodboard/Alamy

255

Essential Question

How can weather affect us?

Go Digital!

Derek Croucher/Alamy

Snow Day!

Talk About It

What are these people doing differently in the snow?

been

They have **been** busy raking.

children

The **children** won their last game of the year.

month

July can be a very hot **month**.

question

Who will answer the **question**?

their

Their dog likes to cool off when it's hot out!

year

It snowed a lot here this **year**.

country

This is a map of our **country**.

gathers

She **gathers** some spring flowers.

Your Turn

COLLABORATE

Read the sentence for each word. Then make up another sentence.

Go Digital! Use the online visual glossary

Silent Letters <u>wr</u>, <u>kn</u>, <u>gn</u>

Sometimes a letter is silent. The letters <u>wr</u>, <u>kn</u>, and <u>gn</u> make the sound you hear at the beginning of **w<u>r</u>ap**, **<u>k</u>now**, and **<u>g</u>nat**.

<u>wr</u>ite	si<u>gn</u>	<u>kn</u>ot
<u>kn</u>ee	<u>gn</u>awed	<u>wr</u>eck
<u>gn</u>at	<u>kn</u>ocking	<u>wr</u>ist
<u>kn</u>ife	<u>wr</u>eath	desi<u>gn</u>

Peter Francis

I knocked a gnat off my wrist.

Another bug gnawed on my knee!

Your Turn

Look for these words with wr, kn, and gn in "Wrapped in Ice."

wrapped	design	know	signs
knocked	Knox	Wright	knock

Genre Realistic Fiction

Essential Question

How can weather affect us?

Read how icy weather affects a neighborhood.

Go Digital!

Peter Francis

262

Wrapped in Ice

The sound of something hitting the window woke Kim up. *Ping! Ping, ping!* "What's that?" Kim asked herself.

Kim peeked outside. The trees were coated with ice. The yard sparkled. The driveway was like a skating rink. Even the car was wrapped in an icy design.

Peter Francis

"Mom, why is everything covered in ice?" Kim wanted to know.

"That's a good **question**," said Mom. "Good thing I'm a science teacher! It's raining. But the air is very cold. So the raindrops freeze when they land on cold surfaces like signs, trees, and roads."

Mom turned on the TV weather. A reporter said, "A winter storm has hit this part of the **country**. Freezing rain is making streets and roads icy. We advise you to stay inside! **Children** can stay home. Schools will be closed."

"We have a snow day!" cried Kim. "You mean an ice day!" laughed Mom.

Peter Francis

Suddenly, all the lights went out!

"I guess some icy tree branches broke," said Mom. "They must have knocked down power lines. We won't have any power until the lines are fixed."

Kim looked worried. But Mom said, "Let's just pretend we are camping!"

Mom lit the logs in the fireplace. Kim got flashlights. They played lots of games. It was fun to eat **their** lunch by the fire.

Then Mom said, "Listen!" The *ping, ping, ping* had stopped!

"The storm must be over!" cried Kim.

Peter Francis

Up and down the street, people came outside. There was so much to do. Everyone worked together. They put sand on the walks. They broke up the ice. Noses got red. Br-r-r-r! The air was very cold.

"I made a fire in the fireplace," Mom called out. "Come in and warm up!"

269

Neighbors came with flashlights and snacks. Ms. Knox brought cider. Mr. Wright told about the **year** it snowed in the **month** of May. Kim told knock-knock jokes.

"It's nice when everyone **gathers** together," said Mom.

Just then, the lights came on. Everyone cheered.

"It's **been** a big day!" smiled Mom. "We were lucky to be cozy and safe."

"We are lucky to have such nice neighbors, too," said Kim. "We turned an ice day into an ice party!"

Make Connections

How does icy weather change Kim and her neighborhood?
Essential Question

Cause and Effect

A **cause** is the reason why something happens. An **effect** is what happens.

Find Text Evidence

Find what caused the raindrops to freeze.

page 265

"Mom, why is everything covered in ice?" Kim wanted to know.

"That's a good **question**," said Mom. "Good thing I'm a science teacher! It's raining. But the air is very cold. So the raindrops freeze when they land on cold surfaces like signs, trees, and roads."

Peter Francis

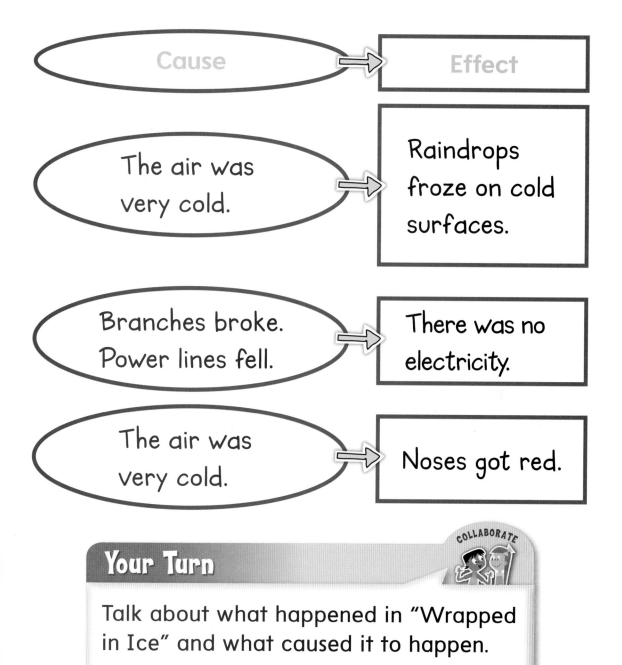

Cause	Effect
The air was very cold.	Raindrops froze on cold surfaces.
Branches broke. Power lines fell.	There was no electricity.
The air was very cold.	Noses got red.

Your Turn

COLLABORATE

Talk about what happened in "Wrapped in Ice" and what caused it to happen.

Go Digital! Use the interactive graphic organizer

Write About the Text

Pages 262–271

Hector

I answered the question: **How are Kim and Mom affected by the weather on pages 266–268?**

Student Model: *Informative Text*

Kim and Mom had a special day because of the weather. There was a winter storm. A news reporter said for everyone to stay inside. Streets were icy and schools were closed.

Main Idea
I used the text to come up with my main idea.

Grammar
<u>Everyone</u> is an **indefinite pronoun**.

Kim and Mom lost power. They pretended they were camping. Mom lit a fire and Kim got flashlights. They played games and ate lunch by the fire. Kim and Mom had so much fun ← staying home together.

Concluding Statement
My last sentence wraps up what I wrote about.

Your Turn
COLLABORATE

How do the people in the town react to the weather in "Wrapped in Ice"?

Go Digital!
Write your response online.
Use your editing checklist.

275

Essential Question

What traditions do you know about?

Go Digital!

Talk About It

What is this boy learning from his grandmother?

(bkgd)©Monalyn Gracia/Corbis; (inset)Jacques Cornell/McGraw-Hill Education

276

Pass It On!

before

They read **before** going to bed.

front

The dog walks in **front** of the girl.

heard

Have you **heard** Dad play?

push

Mom will **push** the sled.

tomorrow

I hope it will be sunny **tomorrow**.

your

I'm glad to meet **your** mom!

difficult

This puzzle is **difficult** to do.

nobody

Nobody is on the porch.

Your Turn

COLLABORATE

Read the sentence for each word. Then make up another sentence.

Go Digital! Use the online visual glossary

(t to b, l to r) Yellow Dog Productions/Getty Images; Profimedia International s.r.o./Alamy; Somos Images/Corbis; ableimages/SuperStock; Purestock/Getty Images; SW Productions/Brand X/Corbis; Jose Luis Pelaez/Iconica/Getty Images; David Papazian/Photographer's Choice RF/Getty Images

Three-Letter Blends

The letters scr, spl, spr, str, thr, and shr make the beginning sounds in **scramble**, **split**, **spring**, **stripes**, **three**, and **shrink**.

scrub	**sprayed**	**street**
splash	**shrink**	**thrilling**
spread	**scream**	**thread**
shriek	**splinters**	**strike**

A stream of water sprayed and splashed us.

The thrill made us shriek and scream.

Your Turn

Look for these words with scr, spl, spr, str, thr, and shr in "A Spring Birthday."

spring	street	sprang
spread	striking	three
split	shrieked	scrambled

Essential Question

What traditions do you know about?

Read about how a family starts a new tradition.

Go Digital!

Hector Borlasca

282

A Spring Birthday

May was a happy time for Marco. It was his birthday month.

"Can I have a party this year?" he asked. "Then my friends can celebrate with me."

"It's our family tradition to have a birthday dinner," said Gram. "**Your** friends can join us. I will make *empanadas* for everyone."

"**Nobody** makes better *empanadas*, Gram!" Marco said. "But it would be fun to do something new this year."

"How about a picnic?" Dad asked. "I **heard** about a nice spot in the park on Elm Street. It's in **front** of the ball field. We can **push** the tables together."

"That sounds like fun," said Marco. "We can have hotdogs, burgers, and Gram's *empanadas*!"

Hector Borlasca

At last, it was the morning of Marco's birthday. He opened his eyes. He saw Mom and Dad and Gram. They were singing the Mexican birthday song, "*Las mañanitas.*" Marco sprang out of bed. He could not wait for his party.

Mom and Dad went shopping **before** the party. First, they got a baseball mitt for Marco. Then they bought a birthday cake and a *piñata*.

Everyone met at the picnic spot. "Happy birthday! *Feliz cumpleaños*, Marco!" they shouted.

Hector Borlasca

Mom hung the *piñata*. Dad spread out the food. There were hotdogs, burgers, and yummy *empanadas*!

After lunch, the children took turns striking the *piñata*. Each one swung three times. The *piñata* was **difficult** to hit! At last it split open. The kids shrieked and scrambled for the treats.

Next Marco opened his gifts. When he saw the baseball mitt, he cried, "Thank you! This is just what I wanted! I can use it in the game **tomorrow**."

When it was time for cake, Marco's family sang the Mexican birthday song again. Marco's friends hummed along. Then Mom taught them the words so they could sing it, too!

"This is the best birthday party I've ever had!" Marco said. "Can we do this again next year?"

"Sure," said Gram. "It's fun to mix the old with the new. A spring picnic can be your birthday tradition."

Make Connections

What traditions do you know about from other places in the world? **Essential Question**

Theme

The **theme** of a story is the message that the author wants to tell readers.

🔍 Find Text Evidence

Find clues that can help you figure out the theme of "A Spring Birthday."

page 285

"It's our family tradition to have a birthday dinner," said Gram. "**Your** friends can join us. I will make *empanadas* for everyone."

"**Nobody** makes better *empanadas*, Gram!" Marco said. "But it would be fun to do something new this year."

Hector Borlasca

Clue

A birthday dinner is the family's tradition.

Clue

Marco's family has a picnic with a *piñata*, *empanadas*, and other kinds of food.

Clue

Marco wants a birthday picnic next year.

Theme

Blend old and new to make a new tradition.

COLLABORATE

Your Turn

Talk about the theme of "A Spring Birthday."

Go Digital! Use the interactive graphic organizer

Pages 282–291

Write About the Text

Kate

I responded to the prompt: **Write a letter from Marco to his parents thanking them for his great birthday.**

Student Model: *Narrative Letter*

Dear Mom and Dad,

This birthday was the best ever! The picnic party was great. I liked that we combined old things and new things.

My friends had a blast at our party in the park. The food was yummy, and the piñata was so much fun!

Vary Sentence Types
I used an exclamatory sentence to show excitement.

Describing Details
I added details about the party.

My favorite birthday gift was
the baseball mitt from you.
Thank you for getting it
for me. It fits perfectly.
I know it will help me be
a better baseball player.

Thanks for the greatest
birthday!

Your son,
Marco

Grammar

The **pronoun** <u>me</u> is used to stand for Marco.

COLLABORATE

Your Turn

Write a letter from Marco to his parents explaining why he wants to start a new tradition. Describe what the new tradition might be.

Go Digital!
Write your response online.
Use your editing checklist.

Essential Question

Why do we celebrate holidays?

Go Digital!

Red, White, and Blue

Talk About It

What are these people celebrating together?

Ron Sherman/Stone/Getty Images

favorite

It's my **favorite** day of the year!

few

A **few** of the apples are green.

gone

All the leaves are **gone**.

surprise

He has a **surprise** for his sister!

wonder

I **wonder** what is up in the tree.

young

The **young** child fell fast asleep.

nation

Our **nation** has 50 states.

unite

We all **unite** to help the earth.

Your Turn

COLLABORATE

Read the sentence for each word. Then make up another sentence.

Go Digital! **Use the online visual glossary**

air, are, ear

The letters air, are, and ear can make the sounds at the end of **fair**, **share**, and **pear**.

air	care	hair
bear	pair	glare
wear	scare	chair
stair	square	aware

Tim Beaumont

A p<u>air</u> of ch<u>air</u>s were at the squ<u>are</u> table.

She likes to w<u>ear</u> a bow in her h<u>air</u>.

Your Turn

Look for these words with <u>air</u>, <u>are</u>, and <u>ear</u> in "Share the Harvest and Give Thanks."

sh<u>are</u>	f<u>air</u>	aw<u>are</u>	comp<u>are</u>
aff<u>air</u>	w<u>ear</u>	p<u>ear</u>s	

TIME FOR KIDS®

Essential Question

Why do we celebrate holidays?

Read about how people celebrate the harvest.

Go Digital!

Share the Harvest and Give Thanks

Each year, farmers pick crops from their fields. This is called the harvest. It marks the end of the growing season—a fun time of the year.

Say Thanks

In our **nation**, families celebrate the harvest in a number of ways. You can eat a harvest dinner at home, or you can go to a fair or festival. Harvest is a time to **unite** with friends and family. It is also a time when people share harvest foods.

Farm stands have harvest fruits and vegetables. These may include pumpkins and apples in the fall and berries and tomatoes in the spring.

All across the United States, people give thanks for the fall harvest. This day is called Thanksgiving. It is on the fourth Thursday in November. Families eat together and show that they are thankful. But are you aware of the very first Thanksgiving?

In 1620, the people we call Pilgrims sailed from England and landed in Plymouth, Massachusetts. The Native Americans there taught the Pilgrims which crops to plant.

The first Thanksgiving in our nation was in 1621. The Pilgrims who had come to America had a feast to show thanks for the harvest. They ate duck, deer, corn, and squash. Can you compare that to a meal today?

Today, families still give thanks with a feast. But they may eat such **favorite** foods as turkey, corn, and green beans. People like to enjoy the harvest foods before they are **gone**.

Many families eat a special meal on Thanksgiving. Foods that are harvested in the fall may be part of the celebration.

Festivals and Fairs

In many states, Thanksgiving is a fun affair! Some places hold big parades where people march, sing, and dance. At one parade, **young** actors wear costumes. They act out the first Thanksgiving. That is so you can see what harvest was like so many years ago.

In Plymouth, the city of the first Thanksgiving, some people dress up like Pilgrims and Native Americans.

At the Kentucky Harvest Festival, the corn crop is the star. Kids have a contest to peel the most ears of corn. Families join teams to play a Cornhole Toss game. The teams toss a **few** bags filled with corn kernels. They follow rules to score. The winning team gets a **surprise**!

A bean-bag toss game is popular at Kentucky and Ohio harvest festivals. Players pitch their corn bags and try to get them into a hole.

Stan Rohrer/Alamy

309

Kwanzaa is also a harvest celebration. Kwanzaa means "first fruits." At this time, people give thanks for crops such as corn, apples, and pears.

In some places, pumpkins are a BIG deal! Large pumpkins are dug out and used as boats. After the race the pumpkins are used for compost, or to make new dirt.

Kwanzaa begins on December 26. It celebrates the harvest of Africa. Many people in the United States celebrate Kwanzaa traditions.

Row, row, row your pumpkin! These giant pumpkins make a splash at Oregon's Giant Pumpkin Race.

Key

 Pumpkin Race in Oregon

Corn Festivals in
Kentucky and Ohio

Pilgrims at the First
Thanksgiving in
Massachusetts

Across the nation, people celebrate the harvest. At home or with others, it is no **wonder** that harvest is a fun time for all!

Make Connections

How do you celebrate the harvest? **Essential Question**

George Hamblin

Author's Purpose

An **author's purpose** is the reason why an author writes a selection.

 Find Text Evidence

Find a clue to help you understand the author's purpose.

page 306

The first Thanksgiving in our nation was in 1621. The Pilgrims who had come to America had a feast to show thanks for the harvest. They ate duck, deer, corn, and squash. Can you compare that to a meal today?

Clue
The first Thanksgiving feast was in 1621 to show thanks for the harvest.

Clue
Today people still have feasts on Thanksgiving. There are also parades, fairs, and festivals.

Author's Purpose
To give information about the first Thanksgiving and how it is celebrated today.

Your Turn

COLLABORATE

Talk about the author's purpose for writing "Share the Harvest and Give Thanks."

Go Digital! *Use the interactive graphic organizer*

Write About the Text

Pages 302–311

Grace

I answered the question: **In your opinion, what is the most interesting way people celebrate the harvest?**

Student Model: *Opinion*

I think the most interesting way people celebrate the harvest is at a festival. There are so many things to see and do. People can sing, march, and dance in a parade! People can also dress up and wear costumes.

Author's Voice
I showed my feelings and excitement.

314

(l)Thomas Northcut/Photodisc/Getty Images; (b)Stan Rohrer/Alamy

Grammar

The **adverb** <u>quickly</u> tells how I can peel ears of corn.

The corn festival looks very fun. I would like to race to peel ears of corn. I know that I could do it quickly! My family likes to play Cornhole Toss. I know we could win a prize! A festival brings people together to have fun and celebrate the harvest the best.

Concluding Statement My last sentence wraps up my response.

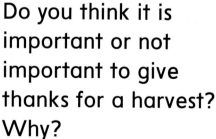

Your Turn

COLLABORATE

Do you think it is important or not important to give thanks for a harvest? Why?

Go Digital!
Write your response online.
Use your editing checklist.

315